MEXICAN
FOOD AND DRINK

Manuel Alvarado

FOOD AND DRINK

British Food and Drink
Chinese Food and Drink
French Food and Drink
Greek Food and Drink
Indian Food and Drink
Italian Food and Drink

Japanese Food and Drink
Mexican Food and Drink
Middle Eastern Food and Drink
North American Food and Drink
Russian Food and Drink
Spanish Food and Drink

Editor: Jillie Norrey
Consultant: Vivien von Son

First published in 1988 by
Wayland (Publishers) Limited
61 Western Road, Hove
East Sussex BN3 1JD, England

British Library Cataloguing in Publication Data

Alvarado, Manuel
  Mexican food and drink.—
  (Food and drink).
  1. Cookery, Mexican—Juvenile
  literature   2. Beverages—Mexico
  —Juvenile literature
  I. Title   II. Series
  641'.0972   TX716.M4

ISBN 1–85210–028–1

Typeset by DP Press, Sevenoaks
Printed in Italy by G. Canale & C.S.p.A., Turin
Bound in France by A.G.M.

Note: *An attempt has been made in the recipes to adhere to current nutritional guidelines which recommend a reduction of salt, sugar and saturated fats, and an increase in fibre in the diet.*

Cover *A large variety of prepared foods are sold on the streets of Mexico. These women are making* tortillas.

Contents

Mexico and its people

When asked, on his return to Spain, to describe the region which was to become the country of Mexico, the conquistador, Hernan Cortes, is said to have picked up a piece of paper, crumpled it in his hand and thrown it on a table, declaring it to offer a relief map of the country. With the exception of the small southern area of Yucatan, Mexico is an extremely mountainous country with high peaks and huge plateaux.

The country occupies the southern part of North America, but because it is historically and politically connected with the Spanish Empire, it is always grouped as one of the Latin American countries. After Brazil and Argentina, Mexico is the third largest Latin American country and has the second largest population (75 million), the majority of whom speak Spanish.

Half of Mexico is within the tropics and the country has very long eastern (the Atlantic) and western (the Pacific) coastlines. Two huge mountain ranges run down each side of the country. In between lies a very high plateau

A woman selling her vegetable produce at the famous market of Oaxaca in southern Mexico.

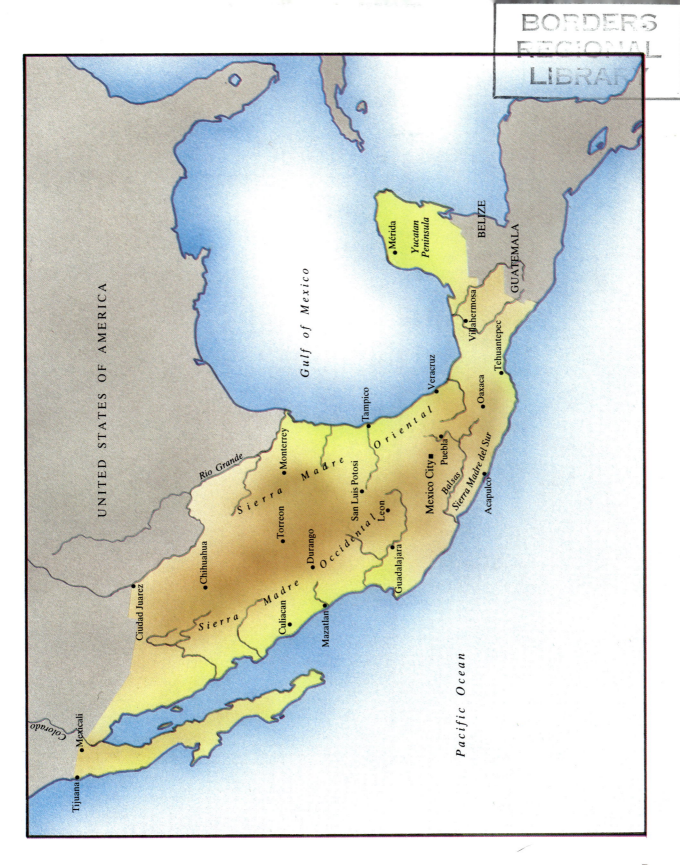

UNITED STATES OF AMERICA

Gulf of Mexico

Yucatan
Peninsula

Mérida

BELIZE

GUATEMALA

Villahermosa

Tehuantepec

Veracruz

Oaxaca

Tampico

Sierra Madre Oriental

Rio Grande

Monterrey

Mexico City

Puebla

Torreon

San Luis Potosi

Balsas

Sierra Madre del Sur

Acapulco

Chihuahua

Durango

Sierra Madre Occidental

Leon

Guadalajara

Culiacan

Ciudad Juarez

Sierra Madre

Mazatlan

Pacific Ocean

Colorado

Mexicali

Tijuana

The volcanoes of Popocatepetl and Iztaccihuatl which overlook Mexico City.

region. To the north of the country there is a 2 500 km border with the USA and to the south, Mexico borders the Central American countries of Guatemala and Belize.

This geographical position and structure means that Mexico has one of the most varied climatic zones in the world: the long, low-lying coastal lands form the Tierra Caliente or tropical regions; the higher regions up to the plateau level (1 800 m) form the Tierra Templada or temperate region; and above that level is the Tierra Fria or cold region. The mountains in Mexico can reach over 5 000 m above sea level and the two volcanoes, Popocatepetl and

Iztaccihuatl, which overlook Mexico City, are permanently snow-covered.

As a result of this wide range of climates, the country grows a vast selection of fruit and vegetables, and can support huge cattle-rearing ranches in the northern grasslands. Mexico also has a very large fishing industry. At the same time, however, this agriculturally rich country is also very poor. One third of the poor rural peasants work the land and roughly the same proportion have moved to the cities where they lead, in many cases, an even poorer existence. But there is always the hope that the problems caused by inflation and the national debt will eventually be solved in Mexico.

Present-day Mexico, or rather the Estados Unidos Mexicanos (the United States of Mexico) is a federal republic of thirty-one states and one federal district, Mexico City itself. The ruling government party, the Institutional Revolutionary Party (PRI), has been in power since 1929. However, the country has a very ancient and magnificent history stretching back long before the birth of Jesus.

The indigenous civilizations of pre-Columbian Mexico inhabited

The National Cathedral of Mexico City in La Playa Mayor de la Constitucion.

the land for a thousand years before the arrival of Hernan Cortes in 1519 and there were many great cultures which have left behind huge archaeological remains. Some of the pyramids are equal in size to those found in Egypt, and cultures such as that of the Mayas (who lived in southern Mexico and Guatemala) had more advanced astronomical and mathematical knowledge than the rest of the world at that time. Gold, the great measure of wealth in Europe, existed in vast quantities. But cacao, from which we make chocolate today, was considered of far more value and was used as a form of money. Moctezuma, an Aztec emperor, is said to have had many treasure rooms in his palace filled with nothing but cacao beans.

The arrival of the Spanish conquistadores, at the beginning of the sixteenth century, led to the end of these powerful cultures. The Spaniards subjugated the people, took their land and stole their gold ornaments (which were melted down and shipped back to Europe). They also destroyed many of their writings and buildings including those in the capital of the Aztecs, Tenochitlan, which is now covered by modern Mexico City. Today

The Aztec's Pyramid of the Moon at Teotihucan, just outside Mexico City.

An illustration based on a native painting of an Aztec encounter with the Spanish conquistadores.

most of what we know about the ancient Mayas has simply been handed down by word of mouth and their language is only spoken by a small number of people in Yucatan.

During 300 years of direct rule from Spain, the population became increasingly Christian and Spanish-speaking. In 1821, independence was finally achieved. The nineteenth century was a turbulent period politically for the country. There were wars with the United States (which led to Mexico having to give up Texas, California and New Mexico) and, in 1862, the French invaded and installed the Austrian Archduke Ferdinand Maximilian Joseph of Hapsburg as emperor of Mexico. The 'empire' collapsed with his execution five years later and the country returned to being a republic under the leadership of Benito Juarez, the only leader of modern times to be directly descended from the indigenous peoples of the region.

Juarez attempted to return the land to the Mexican people but it was the Mexican Revolution, under the revolutionary leadership of people like Pancho Villa and Emiliano Zapata, that saw the greatest attempt to reform the country's social structure and land system. The Revolution began in 1910 as a result of the corrupt thirty-

One of the leaders of the Mexican revolution, Emiliano Zapata.

year dictatorship of Porfirio Diaz, but it ended in failure with both Villa and Zapata being killed. Nevertheless, the Constitution of 1917 established a democratic parliamentary system which is still in operation today.

This history is significant for Mexican cooking because it begins to explain why the cuisine is so rich and varied. Mexican recipes are unique because they combine the culinary traditions of the indigenous peoples with the influence of Spanish and, later, French cuisine.

When the first conquistadores arrived in what is now Mexico, they came across many plants and foods never before encountered. Tomatoes, potatoes, beans, capiscums (peppers), avocados, chillis, vanilla, maize, cacao (chocolate), peanuts, bananas and many other fruits were all staple foods of the Americas. Turkeys had never been seen before and all these foods were shipped back to Europe and gradually integrated into European cooking. At the same time, the Europeans began to introduce their own favourites such as onions, garlic, wheat, rice, olives, grapes and livestock, like pigs and cattle, which were all unknown in the Americas.

Cooking techniques were also quite different. For example, the people of the Americas boiled, steamed or grilled their food but had no knowledge of frying as they

A native Mexican woman of the Huichol tribe selling dried maize and weavings.

had no vegetable oils or animal fats.

It is important to note that real Mexican cooking is still little known outside the country itself. What often passes for Mexican food in Great Britain, the USA, Canada and Australia should be more correctly called Tex-Mex or Texican food as it is a cuisine of mixed origin coming from the southern states of the USA and is not to be found in Mexico. You will certainly not find *chilli con carne* being cooked in any home or restaurant in Mexico itself!

The production and selling of food

Because of the varied landscape and climate of the country, there is a huge variety of food grown and harvested in Mexico. The long coastline supplies the country with a wide range of fish and shellfish. The low-lying land of the coast is mostly tropical and therefore an abundance of citrus fruits, coconuts, sugar cane, mangoes, paw-paws, avocados and many types of banana grow there. These also grow in the extremely hot, flat southern peninsula which includes the state of Yucatan.

The main crop of the country, however, is maize, from which is made the staple food, the *tortilla*. This is a flat bread unlike the Spanish *tortilla* which is a potato omelette. *Tortillas* are eaten with every meal. Another staple food is the wide range of beans which are also eaten with most meals, particularly red kidney, black, pinto and borlotti beans. The two crops, maize and beans, are very

Examples of three of Mexico's most popular fruits – peaches, pomegranates and mangoes.

economical to cultivate because they can be grown in the same furrow and therefore they make up the staple diet of the majority of the population.

Chilli peppers are an important flavouring element of Mexican dishes, and bananas and plantains (of which there are many different varieties) are important too. In the south, banana and plantain leaves are also used to wrap up food to be cooked.

The rich grasslands of northern Mexico are well suited to raise

A corn field in Yucatan – the most southern, flattest and hottest region of Mexico.

cattle and grow wheat. *Tortillas*, therefore, are often made with wheat, not maize, and far more beef is eaten. Cattle are also bred to provide milk which is used in cheese production.

Further south, pigs, goats, turkeys and chickens are bred for meat. The other main food crops of Mexico are potatoes, tomatoes, rice, tobacco, sugar, coffee and cacao, and these are also produced to the south. Another very important crop is a plant similar to a cactus called the *agave*, and the related *maguey*, from which are made *tequila, mezcal* and *pulque*, the three most popular alcoholic beverages in Mexico (see page 38–9).

However, while the range of crops in Mexico is spectacular, the volume of production is very low. The reasons for this are largely political. The majority of the rural population are poor peasants who do not own the land on which they work. Much of the land is owned and exploited by multi-national food and mineral corporations. If peasants do own the land, it is usually barely enough to support subsistence farming, and only one quarter of the tillable land is used for growing crops. This problem is made worse because there is no irrigation in many areas.

The mountainous terrain makes it difficult to transport food around the country. Most bulk food is

Mestizo (half native, half hispanic) women selling cocks near the town of Otomi.

carried in lorries. Peasant farmers, however, still transport their produce on a *burro* (donkey) or on the bus to the local markets. These markets remain the most important places for the buying and selling of animals, vegetables and fruit. It is not uncommon to see a goat being carried to the market on the roof of a bus!

Large towns, like Guadalajara and Oaxaca, have colourful markets where villagers come to sell their produce. There you can see all the kinds of tomatoes, lettuces, chillis, avocados and bananas imaginable. You may also see poor peasants with perhaps just

A stallholder selling corn-fed chicken, a popular meat in Mexican cooking.

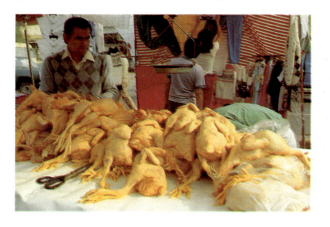

Freshly-barbecued sweetcorn, sprinkled with chilli, can be found all over Mexico City.

a few limes and peppers neatly piled on the floor in front of them. Chickens and turkeys are often sold live as baby chicks, to be reared by a family until fully grown and ready to eat.

In addition, a large range of cooked and prepared food is sold on the streets of Mexico. For example, little stalls sell hot, barbecued sweetcorn sprinkled with chilli, or little paper boxes of fresh fruit salad which are also sprinkled with chilli! Sometimes you can buy some form of *antojitos* (snacks), or ready-made candy floss on street corners. Every time a bus pulls into a village, women with huge platters of wonderful-smelling, freshly-cooked dishes and *tortas* (a snack rather like a *tacos*), gather round to sell their food.

The meals

Although the basic elements of Mexican cooking will be similar for the majority of the population, there are huge differences in what people eat, according to their wealth.

The rural peasant

Peasant women rise before dawn to prepare the *tortillas* and strong black coffee for *desayuno* (breakfast). By late morning the men return from the fields for *almuerzo* (second breakfast) which consists of more *tortillas* and coffee with *frijoles* (beans) and perhaps *biscochos* (sweet buns). After returning to work, *la comida* (lunch) is taken at around 2 pm. This consists of more *tortillas* and *frijoles* with perhaps a *sopa* (soup) and maybe a little meat and *salsa de jitomate* (tomato sauce). A *cerveza* (beer) is more likely to be drunk with *la comida*. After a *siesta*, to

Mayan women making tortillas. *Having ground the maize by hand they make the flour into pancakes and cook them on an open fire.*

A local butcher's shop in Yucatan where a Mayan woman is buying some meat.

avoid the heat of the day, the peasant will return to work and probably will not eat again until late evening when *la cena* (dinner) is eaten. This is a small meal likely to consist again of *tortillas*, *frijoles*, coffee and perhaps fruit.

In addition to this, *antojitos* are often eaten between meals. The men might also go, at some point of the day, to a *pulqueria* to drink a *pulque* (see page 38).

The poor city dweller

The daily meals are similar to those of the rural peasant. The main difference is that *tortillas* are unlikely to be made at home but bought instead from a *tortilla* shop, which mass-produce them, or are delivered to the door. Meat or a *chorizo* (sausage) might be bought on special occasions. However, on festival days, the poor, whether they live in the country or in the city, will prepare a wider range of food and drink.

The middle and upper classes

People with more money are able to enjoy a wonderful and extremely healthy cuisine. *Desayuno* consists of fresh orange juice or half a cantaloup melon, *huevos rancheros* (ranch-style eggs), *biscochos* and black coffee or *chocolate caliente* (hot chocolate) which is especially popular with children. Office workers start at 8 am and *almuerzo* consists of coffee and *biscochos* around 10.30 am.

For office workers in Mexico City, *la comida* can be a very long meal as the lunch break stretches from 1 pm until 4 pm and most people eat out in a restaurant rather than go home. This meal may consist of several courses and will include *sopa aguada* ('wet soup'), *sopa seca* ('dry soup' made of rice or pasta), a meat dish, vegetables, beans and salad, together with *tortillas* and *salsa cruda* (see page 20), and a tropical fruit salad. Many Mexicans prefer to finish their meal with fruit than have a pudding not forgetting the coffee of course! They will have

Mexico City has many restaurants which are popular at lunchtimes with business people.

either single pieces (particularly if they are poor) or they will mix a tropical fruit salad.

At a family *comida* there are many *aguas frescas* (fruit drinks) that may be drunk with the meal. Probably the most common is lemonade which is made with freshly-squeezed lemons (which are very cheap in Mexico), water and sugar. Other *aguas frescas* can be made with fruits such as pineapple, melon or watermelon, mixed together with sugar and water in a blender. In addition, there are more unusual soft drinks such as *agua de horchata*, a mixture of soaked raw rice, cinammon and sugar, blended and strained; *agua de jamaica*, a cold tea-like drink made from sugar and

A mother preparing la cena *in the kitchen of a middle class family in Mexico City.*

a red flower called jamaica; and *agua de tamarindo* made with the pulp of an acid fruit called tamarind, water and sugar.

For people at home, *la merienda* is a light meal taken in the late afternoon or early evening. For office workers, the day finishes at 8 pm when people go home for *la cena* which, like *la merienda*, is a light meal. People generally only have one or other of them. A *margarita*, which is a cocktail made from *tequila*, triple sec and lime, may be drunk before the meal, and either *cerveza* (beer) or, less often, wine during the meal.

National specialities

Certain foods play an important part in most Mexican meals and may be called national specialities. They are described, with recipes, below.

Chillis

There are many types and colours of chilli in Mexico and they are a basic ingredient in many recipes. They can be extremely hot and should be handled with great care.

It is safest if you always wear rubber gloves when touching them. Never put your hands near your face after touching chillis until you have washed them thoroughly in warm, soapy water. When chopping chillis, use a sharp knife and a fork.

First, wash the chillis in cold water, remove the stem and cut them lengthwise. Then, remove the

Making tortillas using a tortilla press to flatten the dough prior to frying.

Fried plantain (a form of banana) encircling a popular egg dish – huevos motuleños.

seeds and the ribs (which are the hottest part), wash the remaining skin and chop them as finely as you can. They are then ready for use. For further information, see 'Types and uses of chillis' at the back of this book.

Tortillas

The Mexican *tortilla* is a small, flat, round, unleavened bread made from maize, which is eaten with all meals. They can now be bought ready-made in tins (and occasionally frozen) but this is an expensive way to eat them and they don't taste so good! It is much better to make your own if you can find the one special ingredient – maize meal flour or *masa harina*. Some specialist food shops now sell it. *Tortillas* are virtually unique among breads for being made with a cooked flour instead of a raw flour.

Tortillas, frijoles refritos and *salsa cruda*, which are essential for many Mexican meals, appear together in the breakfast dish, *huevos rancheros*. To make this famous dish prepare two *tortillas* for each person. Fry two eggs per person until the whites have set but the yolks are still yellow and runny. Place the *tortillas* side-by-side on a plate, place the eggs on top and surround them with *salsa cruda, frijoles refritos* and slices of avocado. Grind black pepper over the eggs and serve with a glass of orange juice.

Salsa Cruda

There are many types of tomato sauce and many variations of each recipe in Mexico. This recipe is for a dish that is also served with almost every meal. It is not cooked and should be prepared just before each meal. You have to eat it all as it does not keep!

You will need:
500 g of tomatoes, finely chopped (leave the skins on)
1 onion, finely chopped
2 tablespoons of chopped, fresh coriander leaves
1 finely chopped chilli (or more according to how hot you like the sauce to be)
Ground black pepper
A little water

What to do:
Simply mix all the ingredients together and place on the table in a small bowl.

Tortillas

You will need:
250 g of *masa harina*
250 ml of luke-warm water

What do do:
Mix the two ingredients together in a bowl for about 10 minutes if doing it by hand, or 5 minutes if using a processor. When it is a good consistency, holding together well and is neither too wet nor too dry, leave it for 20–30 minutes. (1) Divide the mixture into 16 small balls. Heat a flat, dry, heavy frying pan. In Mexico a peasant would then flatten the ball in their hands until it was a very thin, circular pancake. However, this is a rather difficult operation. (2) Use a *tortilla* press instead. You will find it easier. Place a piece of greaseproof paper on one side of the press. Put the ball of dough in the centre of it, cover it with a second piece of paper, pull the top of the press down and flatten the dough until it is no thicker than a thin coin. (3) Take the circle of dough out of the press, place it on the hot pan and dry-fry it for one minute until the edges begin to curl up. Then turn it over with a palette knife and cook for another minute. When it is done it should be flecked with brown on both sides. (4) Store in a hot oven on a plate, separating each *tortilla* with greaseproof paper and wrapping them all in a tea towel.

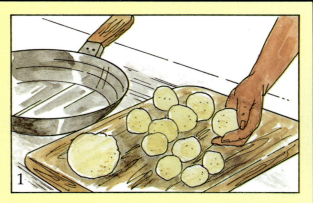

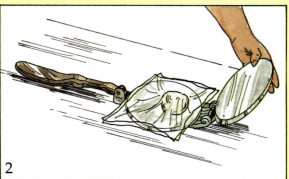

Frijoles refritos

Like many Mexican dishes *frijoles* involve plenty of arm work unless you have a food processor! One of the most common ways of serving them is as *frijoles refritos*. This means refried beans, which is a strange name as they are only fried once!

You will need:

250 g of red kidney/pinto/black beans – whichever are available
½ an onion, finely chopped
1 clove of garlic
a pinch of cumin
2 tablespoons of cooking oil
1 whole green chilli, finely chopped

What to do:

Wash the beans carefully, place them in a bowl with plenty of water and leave them to soak overnight. (1) The next day drain them (you will find that the beans will have swollen in size and there won't be much water left). (2) Place them in a pan, cover them with cold water and add the garlic and cumin. Partially cover and boil for 2–3 hours, regularly topping up the pan with boiling water. You should finish cooking them when the beans are tender and you have a thick soup in the pan. Allow them to cool and then drain them. (3) Place the beans in a food processor and make them into a thick paste. If you do not have a food processor, you can mash them in the pan with a potato masher but this is hard work! (4) Lightly fry the onion and the chilli in the oil and when they are soft (not brown) add the beans. Stir until they are thoroughly mixed and hot. *Frijoles* keep well in the refrigerator and taste even better when reheated the next day!

Regional specialities

The north

Cooking in the north of Mexico, as already indicated, involves wheat, beef and cheese which are not common to the cuisine of the rest of the country. *Tortillas* in the north are often made with wheat instead of maize meal and one of the traditional ways of eating beef is in a dried form called *cecina*. The land is arid and the air very dry and hot so their method of producing *cecina* is not surprising.

A solid chunk of beef is taken and, with a few clever knife cuts, the rancher is able to open up the beef in a long thin concertina-like ribbon of meat. This is sprinkled with salt on both sides, and refolded for two hours so that the meat absorbs it. The ribbon of meat is then unfolded and exposed to the sun until it is fairly dry. It is rubbed with lemon juice and pepper and stretched out in the shade for a further two days after which it is tenderized by pounding it with a stone. Finally, the meat is folded again and stored until it is required for eating. As you can imagine, by this time it has acquired a strong flavour and can be used in many different ways.

The cheese of this area is also strongly flavoured and used primarily in cooking. It is

Cheese is made mainly in the north of the country and is used primarily in cooking.

interesting to note that these three elements, wheat *tortillas*, beef (but not *cecina* which is impossible to buy outside of northern Mexico) and cheese are the key ingredients used in many of the dishes served in the so-called 'Mexican' fast-food restaurants to be found in the USA, Canada, Australia and Great Britain. The dishes such restaurants offer include *tacos*, *enchiladas*, *tostados* and *quesadillas* which are often referred to as *antojitos* in Mexico.

Enchiladas are rolled *tortillas* which encase a wide variety of fillings. They are covered with a sauce and served garnished with salad or *guacamole* (see page 30) as a

Enchiladas *are made, cooked and sold in the street in all the towns of Mexico.*

dish in itself. While *enchiladas* are traditionally made without meat, almost anything can be used for the filling and they provide a useful dish to make with meat leftovers from the fridge. *Enchilada* means 'chillied up' so that chillis must always be included when making this dish! The following recipe is an example of the type of *enchilada* which might be eaten in a restaurant in the north of the country. The recipe includes a simple tomato sauce which can be used both as a filling and as the sauce.

Enchilada with salsa de jitomate

You will need:

475 g of plain flour
100 g of lard (preferably white, cooking Flora)
200 ml of warm water

For the *salsa de jitomate*:
1 onion
1 clove of garlic
1 × 400 g can of tomatoes
1 chilli, finely chopped
1 tablespoon of coriander leaves
ground black pepper

What to do:

Sieve the flour, and cut the lard into small pieces and blend the two together in a bowl. (1) Gradually add the water and keep kneading the dough on a floured work surface until soft and pliable, but not sticky. Cut it into 12–14 pieces and roll each one out with a rolling pin as you would ordinary pastry. (2) You should roll it until it is very thin and then, using a dinner plate, cut it into a neat circle. (3) Meanwhile, heat a heavy, dry frying pan until it is moderately hot and then cook each *tortilla* for approximately half a minute on each side. The *tortilla* should feel pliable and slightly thicker than when it was rolled out. Stack them in a tea cloth with greaseproof paper separating each one and place to one side. (4) Purée the sauce ingredients in a food processor or finely chop everything by hand.

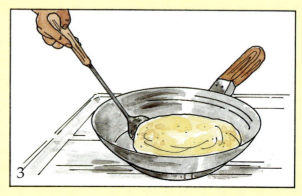

(5) Heat 2 tablespoons of oil in a pan, add the purée and stir the sauce for approximately 5 minutes until the sauce has thickened and it is hot. Season with a little freshly-ground black pepper. Pour oil into the original frying pan in which the *tortillas* were cooked until it is about ½ cm deep. Allow the oil to become moderately hot (it mustn't be too hot or the *tortillas* will go hard and be impossible to roll) and fry each *enchilada* for about 30 seconds on each side. Lift each one out, drain on some kitchen roll and keep them warm in the oven until they are all cooked. (6) When you are ready, place a *tortilla* on a plate, spoon some of the hot *salsa* into the middle, add some grated cheese (preferably something like white cheddar) and freshly-chopped onion and those leftovers if you have any. (7) Roll the *tortilla* up. (8) Do the same for one or two more (depending how greedy you feel!) and then spoon more *salsa*, cheese and onion over the top. *Enchiladas* are tasty served with *frijoles refritos* and shredded white cabbage or lettuce.

Safety note:
Always have an adult standing by to help you when you are cooking with hot oil.

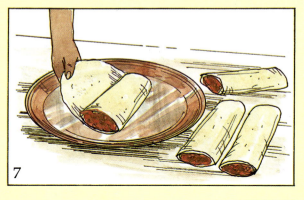

26

The coast

Obviously the coast of Mexico is the best place to find a huge variety of fresh fish and shellfish, and therefore some fine recipes. Probably the most popular fish is red snapper. The most famous fish dish which is made with snapper is *ceviche* – marinated raw fish! As with all other Mexican food, the recipe varies from region to region but basically the fish is filleted, cut into small pieces and soaked overnight in a marinade made from onion, orange juice and lots of lemon juice. It is the acidity of the fruit juices which 'cooks' the fish and, garnished with a tasty sauce, it is a wonderful dish.

The coastline is tropical (or semi-tropical in the north), so this is also the region where an abundance of fruits and vegetables are grown. These include bananas and plantains (a type of banana which is always cooked – either fried or boiled), pineapples, oranges, lemons, limes, mangoes, and probably the most important one of all for Mexican cuisine, avocados. It is estimated that the avocado consumption in Britain amounts to an average of every person eating one avocado a year – in Mexico the average is two per person every

Fresh fish is readily available even in the centre of Mexico City.

single day of the year!

Avocado trees are very beautiful and there are many types of avocado. The best, in terms of flavour, are the small, almost black ones called *paguas*; the large green ones can be watery and tasteless. It is also an extremely versatile fruit because every part of the smallest Mexican variety can be used. The flesh, the skin and the leaves can all be eaten, and a small amount of the stone grated on to *enchilada* sauce is delicious.

In Mexico avocados accompany most meals. They can be sliced

A typical scene of fishermen working in the harbour of Progreso in Yucatan.

and added to salads, placed on top of a cooked stew or eaten with vinaigrette or seafood, as is increasingly common in Europe. They can also be used to fill *tacos* for picnics or, in its most famous form, avocados are made into a dip called *guacamole*. Apart from using them in different ways in soup, the one thing you cannot really do is cook avocados because they become very bitter.

There are many ways to make

guacamole but the following recipe is typical. Some people leave the chillis out but it does taste better with them! Firstly, it is essential to ensure that the avocados are ripe. They will rarely be ripe in the shop or market so make sure that you buy them two or three days in advance and then keep them somewhere warm at home. They are ripe when they no longer feel hard and 'give' slightly when you press your thumbs into the top end.

Secondly, remember that once you cut them open the flesh begins to turn black so, for the best results, you should make this dish just before you intend to eat it.

Avocados are one of Mexico's staple foods. Here a guacomole *has been mixed using* molcajete *and* tejolote *(pestle and mortar).*

Guacamole

You will need:

2 ripe avocados
a little lemon juice
2 fresh tomatoes, finely chopped
½ an onion, finely chopped
1 chilli, finely chopped
2 tablespoons of finely-chopped fresh
  coriander

What to do:

Mix together all the ingredients, apart from the avocados, in a bowl and sprinkle with a little lemon juice. (1) Cut the avocados in half, remove the stones and scoop out the flesh with a spoon, making sure to scrape the skins dry. Mash the flesh with a fork and add it to your mixture. (2) Mix everything well, making sure that you don't make it too smooth. The texture should be a little coarse which is why it is not a good idea to use a processor for this dish. Serve it as an accompaniment to a meal or, better still, as a lovely starter. (3) Spoon it into a serving bowl, sprinkle some chopped coriander over it and serve with tortilla chips which can be used to scoop out the *guacamole*.

The south

The cuisines of southern Mexico are the most exotic and tropical. The central southern state of Oaxaca, for example, is famous for its food markets and its very colourful dishes. *Tamales* are a type of steamed, corn dumpling stuffed with a wide variety of meats and chillis. In the north they are wrapped in corn husks, but in the southern parts of Mexico they are wrapped in banana leaves.

To the south of Oaxaca is an interesting, small town called Tehuantepec where the indigenous peoples still maintain a semi-matriarchal society. This means that it is the women who go out to work and the men stay at home, looking after the children and doing the cooking.

However, perhaps the most distinctive of all the regions of Mexico is the peninsula in

Women making tamales *which are stuffed* tortillas *often cooked in banana leaves.*

the extreme south-east of the country. This area contains the state of Yucatan which has the most powerful indigenous culture remaining from before the Spanish conquest and also the most distinctive cuisine in Mexico. The area is the flattest and lowest part of the country and is covered with tropical rainforests and swamps. Until modern highways were built, one could only reach the region by sea or by air. The descendants of possibly the greatest of all the pre-Columbian civilizations, the Maya,

The beautiful Mayan Pyramid of the Magician at Uxmal in the southern province of Yucatan.

still maintain a powerful cultural identity. There are approximately 2 million descendants of the Maya living in this region and in neighbouring Guatemala. They still speak their own language and cook their traditional dishes.

Fruit and fish are both plentiful and feature strongly in Mayan cooking but the most famous range of meat or poultry dishes are called *pibil* which indicates that they have been steamed in a pit called a *pib*. *Pibs* are made by digging a hole in the ground and filling it with red-hot stones. Then the meat is seasoned and wrapped in banana leaves and placed on the stones. This is a lot of work! Fortunately, however, a version of *pollo pibil* (chicken *pibil*), which is almost as good, can be made in an ordinary domestic oven. The chicken is marinaded for 24 hours so you have to start the day before you wish to eat this dish.

The unusual element of the recipe for *pollo pibil* is *annato*. *Annato* (or *achiote*) is the mild, red-orange spice which gives this, and many Yucatan dishes, their distinctive colour. Increasingly you can find it in specialist food shops but a tandoori mix, which can be found in Indian grocers, is similar and provides a reasonable substitute.

A Mayan family who live in a traditional-style Yucatan house which has no windows.

Pollo pibil

You will need:
4 chicken quarters
140 ml of fresh orange juice
1 lemon, freshly squeezed
2 cloves of garlic, finely chopped
½ teaspoon of oregano
¼ teaspoon of ground cumin
¼ teaspoon of ground cloves
¼ teaspoon of ground cinnamon
ground black pepper
3 tablespoons of *annato* seeds, liquid
    annato, *achiote* or tandoori mixture

What to do:
(1) Combine all the herbs and spices and the juices, preferably in a blender or processor, until they form a smooth paste and then pour it over the chicken pieces which you have placed in a bowl. (2) Rub the chicken with it to make sure it is all covered, cover the bowl and place it in the refrigerator for 24 hours perhaps turning the chicken a couple of times. The next day pre-heat your oven to Gas Mark 3 160°C/320°F and take the chicken out of the fridge. (3) Wrap each piece of chicken securely in a piece of kitchen foil ensuring that plenty of marinade is sealed in with the chicken, and place them in a baking dish. In some South-East Asian shops it is now possible to find banana leaves which would be better to use, but they are more difficult to tie securely! Put the dish in the oven for approximately 2 hours after which the meat should be so tender it will fall off the bone. (4) Before serving, take the chicken out of the wrapping, and place it on a serving dish. You can eat the dish with *tortillas* and *frijoles*, or with boiled rice if you prefer.

A street stall holder selling paper 'cornets' of mixed fruit salad sprinkled with chilli.

Many Mexicans finish their meal with a tropical fruit salad, especially in a state like Yucatan where fruit is so abundant. Obviously, fresh fruit salad can be made with any fruits, and in any proportions. Experiment and make your own recipes up. However, to give it a tropical flavour, try using cantaloup melons, watermelons, mangoes, pineapples, oranges, grapes and bananas. Add chilli powder to be genuinely Mexican.

Because of this range of fruit there are juice bars right across Yucatan with spectacular displays of tropical fruits. Any combination will be squeezed or liquidized for the customer to drink.

Drinks

In a hot country, drinks are always going to be an important part of the culture. As already mentioned, fruit juices are very popular in the south and coffee is drunk everywhere. However, a drink which the people from this part of the world can be said to have invented is now a world-wide favourite – *chocolate caliente* or hot chocolate.

Chocolate caliente is a delicious version of hot chocolate and was,

A stall in Mexico City which sells a wide range of aguas frescas. These are freshly made using fruits such as lemons, pineapples, and melons mixed with sugar and water.

Chocolate caliente

You will need:
100 g of plain, dark chocolate broken
   into small pieces
550 ml of skimmed milk
2 or 3 drops of vanilla essence
a pinch of cinnamon
a pinch of ground cloves

What to do:
Combine the ingredients in a saucepan
and heat gently stirring all the time. (1)
Do not allow it to boil but, when it is hot,
whisk the drink (in Mexico the drink is
whipped with a beautiful wooden
implement called a *molinillo*) and then
pour it into the cups. (2) If you wish,
sprinkle a little more cinnamon over the
top. If you must, add sugar to taste when
stirring the drink in the pan!

before the arrival of the Spaniards, literally the drink of kings. It would have been made with water, as milk was then unknown in the Americas although today it is almost always made with milk.

The traditional alcoholic drink of pre-Columbian Mexico was *pulque* which is made from the sap of a cactus plant called the *maguey*. It is allowed to ferment, is slightly stronger than beer and is a foamy, milky drink with a taste that has been described as 'sour milk mixed with a bit of gunpowder and cheese'! It is best drunk at the ranch where it was made or in a local *pulqueria* but it is really only drunk by the poorer people these days,

especially as it has been replaced in popularity by the good quality beers of Mexico.

In fact, the sap of the *maguey* before it is fermented is called *agua-miel* (water honey) and is very nutritious. It provides an important nutrient in the diet of the poorer people and recently the concentrate of *agua-miel* has begun to be sold in Mexican health shops because of its nutritional value.

Tequila is the internationally-famous Mexican drink which is the distilled juice of another cactus-type plant related to the *maguey*. It is drunk neat and it customary between sips to lick salt and suck slices of lime. *Tequila* forms the basis of many famous cocktails including the *margarita* and the *tequila* sunrise. Another famous Mexican drink is *mezcal* which is made from the *tequila* plant. *Mezcal* is noted for the fact that many of its brands are sold with a dead maggot in the bottle!

Mexico is also a large producer of rum and is an increasingly important wine producer. In fact, you can find almost any drink you want in Mexico!

Right *A worker extracting the sap from the maguey cactus.*
Below *The sap of the maguey cactus which is used to make the alcoholic drink* pulque.

Festive food

Fiestas (festivals) are great occasions in Mexican culture and they are celebrated with music, dancing and wonderful dishes of turkey, pork and other meats. Many of these *fiestas* are based on the religious calendar and the most important of these takes place from 16–24 December.

These nine days represent the nine *posadas* (inns) that Joseph and Mary called at in their search for lodging in Bethlehem. Celebrations are held day and night with dances in public squares and private houses. The dances are interrupted while 'pilgrims' go round singing and holding candles. In most houses an earthenware jar filled with sweets called a *pinata* is hung up on a piece of string. This has to be smashed with a stick by a person wearing a blindfold.

But there are many other reasons for, and ways of, celebrating! In

Right *The beautiful Floating Gardens of Xochimilco where Mexicans love to spend the afternoon.* **Below** *One of the many boats that sell food and drink in the Floating Gardens.*

Mole poblano de guajolote *(turkey in chocolate and chilli sauce)*.

Mexico City itself, for example, there is a beautiful park called the Floating Gardens of Xochimilco where families or groups of office workers can hire a long flat boat with a canopy and a trestle table running down the middle. A man paddles the boat slowly round the network of canals and dozens of little boats come up selling delicious plates of food, and drinks. Others have a photographer who will record the event for them! Finally there are a few large boats where you will be entertained by *Mariarchi* players with traditional songs and tunes. *Mariarchi* players are groups of musicians who play guitars, trumpets, violins and a double bass and who, for a fee, attach themselves to the boat and play. Meanwhile, the party will eat, drink, laugh and even try to dance in the boat!

Two of the most famous Mexican festive dishes are *mancha manteles de cerdo* (meaning, the pork that stains the tablecloth) and *mole poblano de guajolote* (turkey in chocolate and chilli sauce!). *Mancha manteles* was traditionally made on Corpus Christi day and there are many versions of this complicated dish. Its ingredients can include pork, chicken, herbs, almonds, sesame seeds, tomatoes, onions, courgettes, cinammon, chillis and various fruits.

Mole poblano is one of the great national dishes of Mexico and some people believe the recipe was passed down by God to the nuns in the Convent of Santa Rosa, Puebla, during the sixteenth century. However, it quite certainly pre-dates the arrival of the Spaniards and was probably a royal fiesta dish because it is so complicated to make. The sauce alone contains twenty-nine ingredients and it can take three days to prepare!

The word *mole* comes from the Aztec *molli* meaning 'sauce', and the amount of chocolate it contains is tiny and cannot be tasted. However, the chocolate blends with the other ingredients to bring out the flavour. Because it is so complicated to make, the following recipe is a simplified version. In the USA you can buy packet versions of the *mole* but it is more fun to try and make it yourself.

Mole poblano

You will need:

2 kg of turkey pieces
4 cloves of garlic, finely chopped
1 large onion, sliced
100 g of raisins
70 g of almonds
30 g of sesame seeds
1 tablespoon of chopped coriander
250 g of tomatoes
1 tortilla, cut into pieces
¼ teaspoon each of cumin, cloves,
   cinnamon and aniseed
8 dried *ancho* chillis
30 g of grated plain chocolate
ground black pepper
1 chicken stock cube

What to do:

Wash the turkey pieces, dry them and place them in a deep pan in which you have poured and heated enough cooking oil to cover the bottom. (1) Brown the turkey on all sides, remove the pan from the heat, take out the turkey pieces and set them to one side on a plate. Keep the oil. (2) Put the next 8 ingredients into a processor and blend until it forms a smooth paste. Add the rest of the ingredients except the last and continue to blend. (3) Return the pan with the oil to the heat, pour in the mixture and fry it for 5 minutes on a very low heat. Keep stirring it to avoid burning. Dissolve the chicken stock cube in ½ litre of boiling water and pour this into the pan. Finally add the turkey pieces, cover the pan and simmer over a low heat for 30 minutes. (4) To serve, take the turkey out of the pan and place on a dish, pouring the sauce over the pieces. Accompany the dish with boiled rice, *frijoles*, *tortillas*, and a green salad.

Types and uses of chillis

There are over a hundred different types of chillis to be found in Mexico and they are sold in three basic forms – fresh, dried and bottled. They are related to the large green/red/yellow peppers (or capiscums) which are now quite common in Europe, Australia, Canada and the USA. In Mexico white, brown and yellow chillis can be found, as well as green and red ones, and they range in flavour from fairly mild to scorching hot!

Before using any of the chillis listed below, please make sure to follow the instructions about the use of chillis on page 19.

Also, while you might occasionally meet someone who nibbles chillis, do not do this yourself because the burning sensation it causes in your mouth can last for days!

There are nearly one hundred varieties of chilli. This stall sells over thirty kinds.

Bottled or canned chillis

Serranos or *jalapeños* chillis are often found bottled or canned in brine and many Mexican families place a small bowl of them on the table to accompany a meal. If used for cooking they should be carefully washed in cold water to remove the brine.

Fresh chillis

The main chillis used are *serranos*, *jalapeños*, *poblanos*, *cayenne*, and *habaneros*, but in Europe only three main types are usually found – very small, thin green (and often faintly red) ones which are extremely hot; a milder, larger and fleshier chilli with the same pointed shape; and a round Chinese lantern-shaped chilli which can be red or yellow and is often called a 'Scotch Bonnet'. This last one is lethal!

Dried chillis

The main dried chillis are the *ancho*, *mulatto*, *pasillo*, *chipotle* and *guajillo*. The first two in this list are the most commonly found outside Mexico and look very similar, with *anchos* being a dark, burnt-red colour and *mulattos* being just slightly darker. They are sold whole or crushed. Depending on the dish, dried chillis can be used by placing crushed ones in a sauce as it is cooking, or whole ones can be soaked in boiling water for 30 minutes before use.

Glossary

Acidity Having a sour taste; having a high acid (as opposed to alkaline) content.

Americas The continent which includes North, South and Central America.

Conquistadores Spanish adventurers, who adopted 'titles' and led groups of mercenaries to the 'New World' to take over lands and make their fortunes.

Descendants The children and their children and so forth of a family or a nation.

Dictatorship Where one person rules a country absolutely without having been democratically elected, and for an unspecified length of time.

Federal republic A territory where several states form a unified country but where each state remains independent in terms of internal and domestic affairs.

Hybrid The offspring of two animals or plants of different species or varieties.

Indigenous Native to, or originating from, a particular region of the world.

Irrigation To provide adequate watering systems (usually via means of artificial channels) for land where the rainfall is normally low.

Latin America Those areas of the Americas whose official languages are Spanish and Portuguese.

Moors People of the Muslim religion who are mixed Berber and Arab and who come from north-west Africa.

Peninsula An area of land which is surrounded on three sides by water and where the fourth side is attached to a larger land mass.

Plateau A flat region high above sea level.

Pre-Columbian Relating to the Americas before they were 'discovered' by Christopher Columbus in 1492.

Siesta A period when, in hot countries, people rest during the heat of the day when it is too hot to work.

Staple A basic element in the diet of a nation.

Subjugate When one group dominates another group, forcing it to do as it is told.

Subsistence farming Farming carried out by a person or a family who are only able to afford to grow enough food to feed themselves and do not grow any surplus for sale to others.

Temperate region An area where the weather and the temperature is moderate – neither very hot nor very cold.

Triple Sec An orange-flavoured liqueur.

Unleavened A dough which does not include yeast and therefore does not rise when baked.

Versatile Able to do many things.

Picture acknowledgements

The publishers would like to thank the following for their permission to reproduce copyright pictures: Anthony Blake 35; Mary Evans Picture Library 9 (both); Tony Morrison/South American Pictures 6, 13 (top), 31; Topham Picture Library 4, 10; Wayland Picture Library 18, 44; ZEFA *cover*. **All other photographs were taken by John Wright**. The map on page 5 is by Thames Cartographic. All step-by-step recipe illustrations are by Juliette Nicholson.

Further reading

Coronado, Rosa, *Cooking the Mexican Way* (Lerner, 1982)

Howard, John, *Mexico – The Land and its People* (Macdonald Educational, 1976)

Kennedy, Diana, *The Cuisines of Mexico* (Harper and Row, 1986)

Kennedy, Diana, *The Tortilla Book* (Harper and Row, 1975)

Kennedy, Diana, *Mexican Regional Cooking* (Harper and Row, 1984)

Leonard, Jonathan Norton, *Latin American Cooking* (Time Life, 1970)

Nichols, Lourdes, *Cooking the Mexican Way* (Sainsbury, 1985)

Nichols, Lourdes, *Mexican Cookery* (Collins, 1984)

Ortiz, Elizabeth Lambert, *The Book of Latin American Cooking* (Robert Hale, 1984)

Scheer, Cynthia, *Mexican Cooking Class Cookbook* (Windward, 1984)

Somonte, Carlos, *We Live in Mexico* (Wayland, 1984)

Wallace, George and Inger, *The Mexican Cook Book* (Nitty Gritty, 1971)

For teachers and parents

Galeano, Eduardo, *Open Veins of Latin America* (Monthly Review, 1973)

Lewis, Oscar *Five Families: Mexican Case Studies in the Culture of Poverty* (Basic, 1959)

Lewis, Oscar *Pedro Martinez: A Mexican Peasant and His Family* (Panther, 1969)

Lewis, Oscar *The Children of Sanchez* (Penguin, 1964)

Sanderson, Stephen E., *The Transformation of Mexican Agriculture* (Princeton, 1986)

Index